Data Quality Requirements Analysis and Modeling

December 1992   WP #3515-93
CISL WP# 92-04

Richard Y. Wang
M. P. Reddy
H. B. Kon

Sloan School of Management, MIT

MASSACHUSETTS
INSTITUTE OF TECHNOLOGY
50 MEMORIAL DRIVE
CAMBRIDGE, MASSACHUSETTS 02139

To appear in the Journal of Decision Support Systems (DSS)
Special Issue on Information Technologies and Systems

Data Quality Requirements Analysis
and Modeling

December 1992   WP #3515-93
                              CISL WP# 92-04

Richard Y Wang
M. P Reddy
H B Kon

Sloan School of Management, MIT

* see page bottom for complete address

Richard Y. Wang E53-317
M. P Reddy E53-322
Henry B Kon E53-322

Sloan School of Management
Massachusetts Institute of Technology
Cambridge, MA 01239

To appear in the Journal of Decision Support Systems (DSS)
Special Issue on Information Technologies and Systems

Toward Quality Data: An Attribute-Based Approach

Richard Y. Wang
M P Reddy
Henry B Kon

November 1992

(CIS-92-04, revised)

Composite Information Systems Laboratory
E53-320, Sloan School of Management
Massachusetts Institute of Technology
Cambridge, Mass. 02139
ATTN: Prof Richard Wang
(617) 253-0442
Bitnet Address rwang@sloan mit edu

ACKNOWLEDGEMENTS   Work reported herein has been supported, in part, by MIT's International Financial Service Research Center and MIT's Center for Information Systems Research. The authors wish to thank Stuart Madnick and Amar Gupta for their comments on earlier versions of this paper   Thanks are also due to Amar Gupta for his support and Gretchen Fisher for helping prepare this manuscript

Toward Quality Data: An Attribute-Based Approach

1.   Introduction

Organizations in industries such as banking, insurance, retail, consumer marketing, and health care are increasingly integrating their business processes across functional, product, and geographic lines   The integration of these business processes, in turn, accelerates demand for more effective application systems for product development, product delivery, and customer service (Rockart & Short, 1989)   As a result, many applications today require access to corporate functional and product databases   Unfortunately, most databases are not error-free, and some contain a surprisingly large number of errors (Johnson, Leitch, & Neter, 1981)   In a recent industry executive report, *Computerworld* surveyed 500 medium size corporations (with annual sales of more than $20 million), and reported that more than 60% of the firms had problems in data quality [1] *The Wall Street Journal* also reported that

> Thanks to computers, huge databases brimming with information are at our fingertips, just waiting to be tapped   They can be mined to find sales prospects among existing customers, they can be analyzed to unearth costly corporate habits, they can be manipulated to divine future trends   Just one problem   Those huge databases may be full of junk   In a world where people are moving to total quality management, one of the critical areas is data [2]

In general, inaccurate, out-of-date, or incomplete data can have significant impacts both socially and economically (Laudon, 1986, Liepins & Uppulun, 1990, Liepins, 1989, Wang & Kon, 1992, Zarkovich, 1966)   Managing data quality, however, is a complex task   Although it would be ideal to achieve *zero defect data*,[3] this may not always be necessary or attainable for, among others, the following two reasons

First, in many applications, it may not always be necessary to attain zero defect data.   Mailing addresses in database marketing is a good example   In sending promotional materials to target customers, it is not necessary to have the correct city name in an address as long as the zip code is correct

Second, there is a cost/quality tradeoff in implementing data quality programs   Ballou and Pazer found that "in an overwhelming majority of cases, the best solutions in terms of error rate reduction is the worst in terms of cost" (Ballou & Pazer, 1987)   The Pareto Principle also suggests that losses are never uniformly distributed over the quality characteristics   Rather, the losses are always distributed in such a way that a small percentage of the quality characteristics, "the vital few," always contributes a high percentage of the quality loss   As a result, the cost improvement potential is

---

1   Computerworld, September 28, 1992, p 80-84
2   The Wall Street Journal, May 26, 1992, page B6
3   just like the well publicized concept of *zero defect products* in the manufacturing literature

high for "the vital few" projects whereas the "trivial many" defects are not worth tackling because the cure costs more than the disease (Juran & Gryna, 1980). In sum, when the cost is prohibitively high, it is not feasible to attain zero defect data.

Given that zero defect data may not always be necessary nor attainable, it would be useful to be able to judge the quality of data. This suggests that we tag data with quality indicators which are characteristics of the data and its manufacturing process. From these quality indicators, the user can make a judgment of the quality of the data for the specific application at hand. In making a financial decision to purchase stocks, for example, it would be useful to know the quality of data through quality indicators such as who originated the data, when the data was collected, and how the data was collected.

In this paper, we propose an attribute-based model that facilitates cell-level tagging of data. Included in this attribute-based model are a mathematical model description that extends the relational model, a set of quality integrity rules, and a quality indicator algebra which can be used to process SQL queries that are augmented with quality indicator requirements. From these quality indicators, the user can make a better interpretation of the data and determine the believability of the data. In order to establish the relationship between data quality dimensions and quality indicators, a data quality requirements analysis methodology that extends the Entity Relationship (ER) model is also presented.

Just as it is difficult to manage product quality without understanding the attributes of the product which define its quality, it is also difficult to manage data quality without understanding the characteristics that define data quality. Therefore, before one can address issues involved in data quality, one must define what data quality means. In the following subsection, we present a definition for the dimensions of data quality.

1.1. Dimensions of data quality

Accuracy is the most obvious dimension when it comes to data quality. Morey suggested that "errors occur because of delays in processing times, lengthy correction times, and overly or insufficiently stringent data edits" (Morey, 1982). In addition to defining accuracy as "the recorded value is in conformity with the actual value," Ballou and Pazer defined timeliness (the recorded value is not out of date), completeness (all values for a certain variables are recorded), and consistency (the representation of the data value is the same in all cases) as the key dimensions of data quality (Ballou

2

& Pazer, 1987). Huh et al. identified accuracy, completeness, consistency, and currency as the most important dimensions of data quality (Huh, et al., 1990).

It is interesting to note that although methods for quality control have been well established in the manufacturing field (e.g., Juran, 1979), neither the dimensions of quality for manufacturing nor for data have been rigorously defined (Ballou & Pazer, 1985; Garvin, 1983; Garvin, 1987; Garvin, 1988; Huh, et al., 1990; Juran, 1979; Juran & Gryna, 1980; Morey, 1982; Wang & Guarrascio, 1991). It is also interesting to note that there are two intrinsic characteristics of data quality:

(1)   Data quality is a multi-dimensional concept.

(2)   Data quality is a hierarchical concept.

We illustrate these two characteristics by considering how a user may make decisions based on certain data retrieved from a database. First the user must be able to get to the data, which means that the data must be accessible (the user has the means and privilege to get the data). Second, the user must be able to interpret the data (the user understands the syntax and semantics of the data). Third, the data must be useful (data can be used as an input to the user's decision making process). Finally, the data must be believable to the user (to the extent that the user can use the data as a decision input). Resulting from this list are the following four dimensions: accessibility, interpretability, usefulness, and believability. In order to be accessible to the user, the data must be available (exists in some form that can be accessed); to be useful, the data must be relevant (fits requirements for making the decision); and to be believable, the user may consider, among other factors, that the data be complete, timely, consistent, credible, and accurate. Timeliness, in turn, can be characterized by currency (when the data item was stored in the database) and volatility (how long the item remains valid). Figure 1 depicts the data quality dimensions illustrated in this scenario.

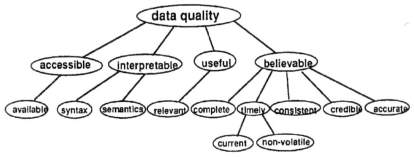

Figure 1: A Hierarchy of Data Quality Dimensions

These multi-dimensional concepts and hierarchy of data quality dimensions provide a conceptual framework for understanding the characteristics that define data quality. In this paper, we focus on interpretability and believability, as we consider accessibility to be primarily a function of the information system and usefulness to be primarily a function of an interaction between the data and the application domain. The idea of data tagging is illustrated more concretely below.

1.2. Data quality: an attribute-based example

Suppose an analyst maintains a database on technology companies. The schema used to support this effort may contain attributes such as company name, CEO name, and earnings estimate (Table 1). Data may be collected over a period of time and come from a variety of sources.

Table 1: Company Information

Company Name	CEO name	Earnings Estimate
IBM	Akers	7
DELL	Dell	3

As part of determining the believability of the data (assuming high interpretability), the analyst may want to know when the data was generated, where it came from, how it was originally obtained, and by what means it was recorded into the database. From Table 1, the analyst would have no means of obtaining this information. We illustrate in Table 2 an approach in which the data is tagged with quality indicators which may help the analyst determine the believability of the data.

Table 2: Company information with quality indicators

Company Name	CEO name	Earnings Estimate
IBM	Akers	7 <source: Barron's, reporting_date: 10-05-92, data_entry_operator: Joe>
DELL	Dell	3 <source: WSJ, reporting_date: 10-06-92, data_entry_operator: Mary>

As shown in Table 2, "7, (source: Barron's, reporting_date: 10-05-92, data_entry_operator: Joe)" in Column 3 indicates that "$7 was the Earnings Estimate of IBM" was reported by the Barron's on October 5, 1992 and was entered by Joe. An experienced analyst would know that Barron's is a credible source; that October 5, 1992 is timely (assuming that October 5 was recent); and that Joe is experienced, therefore the data is likely to be accurate. As a result, he may conclude that the earnings estimate is believable. This example both illustrates the need for, and provides an example approach for, incorporating quality indicators into the database through data tagging.

1.3. Research focus and paper organization

The goal of the attribute-based approach is to facilitate the collection, storage, retrieval, and processing of data that has quality indicators. Central to the approach is the notion that an attribute

4

value may have a set of quality indicators associated with it. In some applications, it may be necessary to know the quality of the quality indicators themselves, in which case a quality indicator may, in turn, have another set of associated quality indicators. As such, an attribute may have an arbitrary number of underlying levels of quality indicators. This constitutes a tree structure, as shown in Figure 2 below.

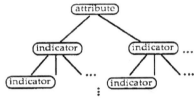

Figure 2: An attribute with quality indicators

Conventional spreadsheet programs and database systems are not appropriate for handling data which is structured in this manner. In particular, they lack the quality integrity constraints necessary for ensuring that quality indicators are always tagged along with the data (and deleted when the data is deleted) and the algebraic operators necessary for attribute-based query processing. In order to associate an attribute with its immediate quality indicators, a mechanism must be developed to facilitate the linkage between the two, as well as between a quality indicator and the set of quality indicators associated with it.

This paper is organized as follows. Section 2 presents the research background. Section 3 presents the data quality requirements analysis methodology. In section 4, we present the attribute-based data model. Discussion and future directions are made in Section 5.

2.   Research background

In this section we discuss our rationale for tagging data at the cell level, summarize the literature related to data tagging, and present the terminology used in this paper.

2.1.   Rationale for cell-level tagging

Any characteristics of data at the relation level should be applicable to all instances of the relation. It is, however, not reasonable to assume that all instances (i.e., tuples) of a relation have the same quality. Therefore, tagging quality indicators at the relation level is not sufficient to handle quality heterogeneity at the instance level.

5

By the same token, any characteristics of data tagged at the tuple level should be applicable to all attribute values in the tuple However, each attribute value in a tuple may be collected from different sources, through different collection methods, and updated at different points in time Therefore, tagging data at the tuple level is also insufficient Since the attribute value of a cell is the basic unit of manipulation, it is necessary to tag quality information at the cell level

We now examine the literature related to data tagging

2.2. Work related to data tagging

A mechanism for tagging data has been proposed by Codd It includes NOTE, TAG, and DENOTE operations to tag and un-tag the name of a relation to each tuple The purpose of these operators is to permit both the schema information and the database extension to be manipulated in a uniform way (Codd, 1979) It does not, however, allow for the tagging of other data (such as source) at either the tuple or cell level

Although self-describing data files and meta-data management have been proposed at the schema level (McCarthy, 1982, McCarthy, 1984, McCarthy, 1988), no specific solution has been offered to manipulate such quality information at the tuple and cell levels

A rule-based representation language based on a relational schema has been proposed to store data semantics at the instance level (Siegel & Madnick, 1991) These rules are used to derive meta-attribute values based on values of other attributes in the tuple However, these rules are specified at the tuple level as opposed to the cell level, and thus cell-level operations are not inherent in the model

A polygen model (poly = multiple, gen = source) (Wang & Madnick, 1990) has been proposed to tag multiple data sources at the cell level in a heterogeneous database environment where it is important to know not only the originating data source but also the intermediate data sources which contribute to final query results. The research, however, focused on the "where from" perspective and did not provide mechanisms to deal with more general quality indicators

In (Sciore, 1991), annotations are used to support the temporal dimension of data in an object-oriented environment However, data quality is a multi-dimensional concept Therefore, a more general treatment is necessary to address the data quality issue More importantly, no algebra or calculus-based language is provided to support the manipulation of annotations associated with the data

6

The examination of the above research efforts suggests that in order to support the functionality of our attribute-based model, an extension of existing data models is required.

2.3. Terminology

To facilitate further discussion, we introduce the following terms:

- An **application attribute** refers to an attribute associated with an entity or a relationship in an entity-relationship (ER) diagram. This would include the data traditionally associated with an application such as part number and supplier.

- A **quality parameter** is a qualitative or subjective dimension of data quality that a user of data defines when evaluating data quality. For example, believability and timeliness are such dimensions.

- As introduced in Section 1, **quality indicators** provide objective information about the characteristics of data and its manufacturing process.[4] Data source, creation time, and collection method are examples of such objective measures.

- A **quality parameter value** is the value determined (directly or indirectly) by the user of data for a particular quality parameter based on underlying quality indicators. Functions can be defined by users to map quality indicators to quality parameters. For example, the quality parameter credibility may be defined as *high* or *low* depending on the quality indicator source of the data.

- A **quality indicator value** is a measured characteristic of the stored data. For example, the data quality indicator source may have a quality indicator value *The Wall Street Journal*.

We have discussed the rationale for cell-level tagging, summarized work related to data tagging, and introduced the terminology used in this paper. In the next section, we present a methodology for the specification of data quality parameters and indicators. The intent is to allow users to think through their data quality requirements, and to determine which quality indicators would be appropriate for a given application.

---

4   We consider an indicator objective if it is generated using a well defined and widely accepted measure.

3.   Data quality requirements analysis

In general, different users may have different data quality requirements, and different types of data may have different quality characteristics. The reader is referred to Appendix A for a more thorough treatment of these issues.

Data quality requirements analysis is an effort similar in spirit to traditional data requirements analysis (Batini, Lenzirini, & Navathe, 1986; Navathe, Batini, & Ceri, 1992; Teorey, 1990), but focusing on quality aspects of the data. Based on this similarity, parallels can be drawn between traditional data requirements analysis and data quality requirements analysis. Figure 3 depicts the steps involved in performing the proposed data quality requirements analysis.

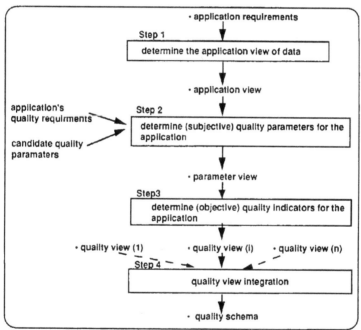

Figure 3: The process of data quality requirements analysis

The input, output and objective of each step are described in the following subsections.

3.1. Step 1: Establishing the applications view

Step 1 is the whole of the traditional data modeling process and will not be elaborated upon in this paper. A comprehensive treatment of the subject has been presented elsewhere (Batini, Lenzirini, & Navathe, 1986; Navathe, Batini, & Ceri, 1992; Teorey, 1990).

For illustrative purposes, suppose that we are interested in designing a portfolio management system which contains companies that issue stocks. A company has a company name, a CEO, and an earnings estimate, while a stock has a share price, a stock exchange (NYSE, AMS, or OTC), and a ticker symbol. An ER diagram that documents the application view for our running example is shown below in Figure 4 .

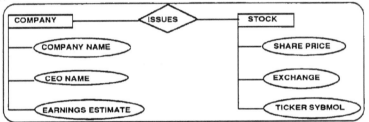

Figure 4: Application view (output from Step 1)

3.2. Step 2: Determine (subjective) quality parameters

The goal in this step is to elicit quality parameters from the user given an application view. These parameters need to be gathered from the user in a systematic way as data quality is a multidimensional concept, and may be operationalized for tagging purposes in different ways. Figure 5 illustrates the addition of the two high level parameters, interpretability and believability, to the application view. Each quality parameter identified is shown inside a "cloud" in the diagram.

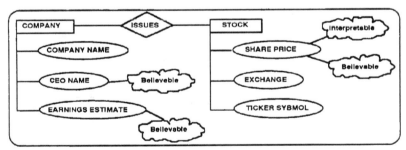

Figure 5: Interpretability and believability added to the application view

9

Interpretability can be defined through quality indicators such as data units (e.g., in dollars) and scale (e.g., in millions). Believability can be defined in terms of lower-level quality parameters such as completeness, timeliness, consistency, credibility, and accuracy. Timeliness, in turn, can be defined through currency and volatility. The quality parameters identified in this step are added to the application view. The resulting view is referred to as the parameter view. We focus here on the stock entity which is shown in Figure 6.

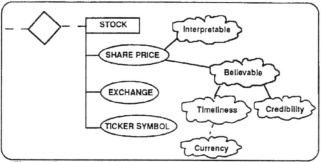

Figure 6: Parameter view for the stock entity (partial output from Step 2)

3.3. Step 3: Determine (objective) quality indicators

The goal in Step 3 is to operationalize the primarily subjective quality parameters identified in Step 2 into objective quality indicators. Each quality indicator is depicted as a tag (using a dotted-rectangle) and is attached to the corresponding quality parameter (from Step 2), creating the quality view. The portion of the quality view for the stock entity in the running example is shown in Figure 7.

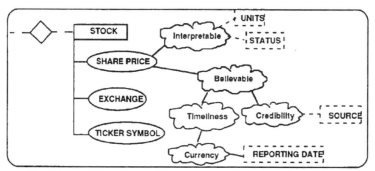

Figure 7: The portion of the quality view for the stock entity (output from Step 3)

10

Corresponding to the quality parameter interpretable are the more objective quality indicators currency units in which share price is measured (e.g., $ vs. ¥) and status which says whether the share price is the latest closing price or latest nominal price. Similarly, the believability of the share price is indicated by the quality indicators source and reporting date.

For each quality indicator identified in a quality view, if it is important to have quality indicators for a quality indicator, then Steps 2-3 are repeated, making this an iterative process. For example, the quality of the attribute Earnings Estimate may depend not only on the first level source (i.e., the name of the journal) but also on the second level source (i.e., the name of the financial analyst who provided the Earnings Estimate figure to the journal and the Reporting date). This scenario is depicted below in Figure 8.

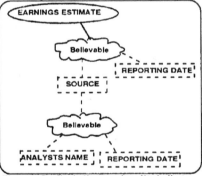

Figure 8: Quality indicators of quality indicators

All quality views are integrated in Step 4 to generate the quality schema, as discussed in the following subsection.

3.4 Step 4: Creating the quality schema

When the design is large and more than one set of application requirements is involved, multiple quality views may result. To eliminate redundancy and inconsistency, these quality views must be consolidated into a single global view, in a process similar to schema integration (Batini, Lenzirini, & Navathe, 1986), so that a variety of data quality requirements can be met. The resulting single global view is called the quality schema.

This involves the integration of quality indicators. In simpler cases, a union of these indicators may suffice. In more complicated cases, it may be necessary to examine the relationships among the indicators in order to decide what indicators to include in the quality schema. For example, it is likely that one quality view may have <u>age</u> as an indicator, whereas another quality view may have <u>creation</u> <u>time</u> for the same quality parameter In this case, <u>creation time</u> may be chosen for the quality schema because age can be computed given current time and creation time

We have presented a step-by-step procedure to specify data quality requirements We are now in a position to present the attribute-based data model for supporting the storage, retrieval, and processing of quality indicators as specified in the quality schema

4.   The attribute-based model of data quality

We choose to extend the relational model because the structure and semantics of the relational approach are widely understood Following the relational model (Codd, 1982), the presentation of the attribute-based data model is divided into three parts   (a) data structure, (b) data integrity, and (c) data manipulation We assume that the reader is familiar with the relational model (Codd, 1970, Codd, 1979, Date, 1990, Maier, 1983)

4.1. Data structure

As shown in Figure 2 (Section 1), an attribute may have an arbitrary number of underlying levels of quality indicators In order to associate an attribute with its immediate quality indicators, a mechanism must be developed to facilitate the linkage between the two, as well as between a quality indicator and the set of quality indicators associated with it This mechanism is developed through the <u>quality key</u> concept In extending the relational model, Codd made clear the need to uniquely identify tuples through a system-wide unique identifier, called the <u>tuple ID</u> (Codd, 1979, Khoshafian & Copeland, 1990) [5] This concept is applied in the attribute-based model to enable this linkage. Specifically, an attribute in a relation scheme is expanded into an ordered pair, called a <u>quality</u> <u>attribute</u>, consisting of the <u>attribute</u> and a <u>quality key</u>

For example, the attribute Earnings Estimate (EE) in Table 3 is expanded into ⟨EE, EE¢⟩ in Table 4 where EE¢ is the quality key for the attribute EE (Tables 3-6 are embedded in Figure 9) This expanded scheme is referred to as a <u>quality scheme</u> In Table 4, ⟨⟨CN, nil¢⟩, ⟨CEO, nil¢⟩, ⟨EE, EE¢⟩⟩ defines a quality scheme for the quality relation Company The "nil¢" indicates that no quality indicators are associated with the attributes CN and CEO, whereas EE¢ indicates that EE has associated quality indicators

Correspondingly, each cell in a relational tuple is expanded into an ordered pair, called a <u>quality cell</u>, consisting of an <u>attribute value</u> and a <u>quality key value</u> This expanded tuple is referred to

---

5   Similarly, in the object-oriented literature, the ability to make references through *object identity* is considered a basic property of an object-oriented data model

12

as a quality tuple and the resulting relation (Table 4) is referred to as a quality relation. Each quality key value in a quality cell refers to the set of quality indicator values immediately associated with the attribute value. This set of quality indicator values is grouped together to form a kind of quality tuple called a quality indicator tuple. A quality relation composed of a set of these time-varying quality indicator tuples is called a quality indicator relation. The quality scheme that defines the quality indicator relation is referred to as the quality indicator scheme.

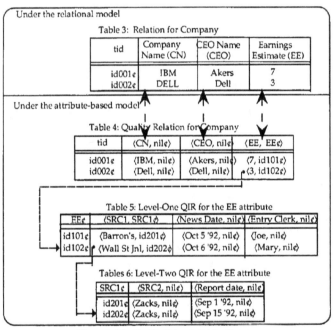

Figure 9: The Quality Scheme Set for Company

The quality key thus serves as a foreign key, relating an attribute (or quality indicator) value to its associated quality indicator tuple. For example, Table 5 is a quality indicator relation for the attribute Earnings Estimate and Table 6 is a quality indicator relation for the attribute SRC1 (source of data) in Table 5. The quality cell (Wall St Jnl, id202¢) in Table 5 contains a quality key value, id202¢, which is a tuple id (primary key) in Table 6.

Let qr_1 be a quality relation and a an attribute in qr_1. If a has associated quality indicators, then its quality key must be non-null (i.e., not "nil¢"). Let qr_2 be the quality indicator relation containing a quality indicator tuple for a, then all the attributes of qr_2 are called level-one quality

13

indicators for a. Each attribute in qr_2, in turn, can have a quality indicator relation associated with it. In general, an attribute can have n-levels of quality indicator relations associated with it, $n \geq 0$. For example, Tables 5-6 are referred to respectively as level-one and level-two quality indicator relations for the attribute Earnings Estimate.

We define a quality scheme set as the collection of a quality scheme and all the quality indicator schemes that are associated with it. In Figure 9, Tables 3-6 collectively define the quality scheme set for Company. We define a quality database as a database that stores not only data but also quality indicators. A quality schema is defined as a set of quality scheme sets that describes the structure of a quality database. Figure 10 illustrates the relationship among quality schemes, quality indicator schemes, quality scheme sets, and the quality schema.

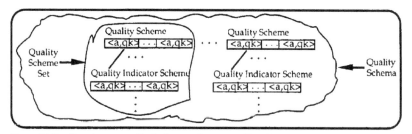

Figure 10 Quality schemes, quality indicator schemes, quality scheme sets, and the quality schema

We now present a mathematical definition of the quality relation. Following the constructs developed in the relational model, we define a domain as a set of values of similar type. Let **ID** be the domain for a system-wide unique identifier (in Table 4, id101e $\in$ ID). Let **D** be a domain for an attribute (in Table 4, 7 $\in$ EE where EE is a domain for earnings estimate). Let **DID** be defined on the Cartesian product D X ID (in Table 4, $\langle 7$, id101e$\rangle \in$ DID).

Let id be a quality key value associated with an attribute value d where $d \in$ D and $id \in$ ID. A **quality relation** (qr) of degree m is defined on the m+1 domains (m>0; in Table 4, m=3) if it is a subset of the Cartesian product:

$$\text{ID X DID}_1 \text{ X DID}_2 \text{ X ... X DID}_m.$$

Let qt be a quality tuple, which is an element in a quality relation. Then a quality relation qr is designated as:

$$qr = \{qt \mid qt = \langle id, did_1, did_2, ..., did_m \rangle \text{ where } id \in \text{ID}, did_j \in \text{DID}_j,\ j = 1, ... ,m\}$$

The integrity constraints for the attribute-based model is presented next.

14

4.2 Data integrity

A fundamental property of the attribute-based model is that an attribute value and its corresponding quality (including all descendant) indicator values are treated as an <u>atomic unit</u>. By atomic unit we mean that whenever an attribute value is created, deleted, retrieved, or modified, its corresponding quality indicators also need to be created, deleted, retrieved, or modified respectively. In other words, an attribute value and its corresponding quality indicator values behave atomically. We refer to this property as the <u>atomicity property</u> hereafter. This property is enforced by a set of quality referential integrity rules as defined below.

<u>Insertion</u>: Insertion of a tuple in a quality relation must ensure that for each non-null quality key present in the tuple (as specified in the quality schema definition), the corresponding quality indicator tuple must be inserted into the child quality indicator relation. For each non-null quality key in the inserted quality indicator tuple, a corresponding quality indicator tuple must be inserted at the next level. This process must be continued recursively until no more insertions are required.

<u>Deletion</u>: Deletion of a tuple in a quality relation must ensure that for each non-null quality key present in the tuple, corresponding quality information must be deleted from the table corresponding to the quality key. This process must be continued recursively until a tuple is encountered with all null quality keys.

<u>Modification</u>: If an attribute value is modified in a quality relation, then the descendant quality indicator values of that attribute must be modified.

We now introduce a <u>quality indicator algebra</u> for the attribute-based model.

4.3. Data manipulation

In order to present the algebra formally, we first define two key concepts that are fundamental to the quality indicator algebra: <u>QI-compatibility</u> and <u>QIV-Equal</u>.

4.3.1. QI-Compatibility and QIV-Equal

Let a_1 and a_2 be two application attributes. Let $QI(a_i)$ denote the set of quality indicators associated with a_i. Let S be a set of quality indicators. If $S \subseteq QI(a_1)$ and $S \subseteq QI(a_2)$, then a_1 and a_2 are defined to be **QI-Compatible** with respect to S.[6] For example, if $S = \{qi_1, qi_2, qi_{21}\}$, then the attributes a_1 and a_2 shown in Figure 11 are QI-Compatible with respect to S. Whereas if $S = \{qi_1, qi_{22}\}$, then the attributes a_1 and a_2 shown in Figure 11 are <u>not</u> QI-Compatible with respect to S.

---

6   We assume that the numeric subscripts (e.g., qi_{11}) map the quality indicators to unique positions in the quality indicator tree.

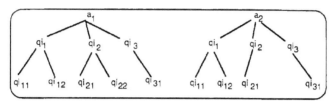

Figure 11: QI-Compatibility Example

Let a_1 and a_2 be QI-Compatible with respect to S. Let w_1 and w_2 be values of a_1 and a_2 respectively. Let $qi(w_1)$ be the value of quality indicator qi for the attribute value w_1 where $qi \in S$ ($qi_2(w_1) = v_2$ in Figure 12). Define w_1 and w_2 to be **QIV-Equal** with respect to S provided that $qi(w_1) = qi(w_2)$ $\forall$ $qi \in S$, denoted as $w_1 =^S w_2$. In Figure 12, for example, w_1 and w_2 are QIV-Equal with respect to $S = \{qi_1, qi_{21}\}$, but **not** QIV-Equal with respect to $S = \{qi_1, qi_{31}\}$ because $qi_{31}(w_1) = v_{31}$ whereas $qi_{31}(w_2) = x_{31}$.

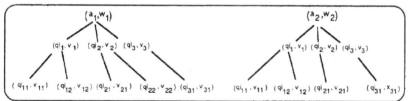

Figure 12: QIV-Equal Example

In practice, it is tedious to explicitly state all the quality indicators to be compared (i.e., to specify all the elements of S). To alleviate the situation, we introduce i-level QI-compatibility (i-level QIV-Equal) as a special case for QI-compatibility (QIV-equal) in which **all** the quality indicators up to a certain level of depth in a quality indicator tree are considered.

Let a_1 and a_2 be two application attributes. Let a_1 and a_2 be QI-Compatible with respect to S. Let w_1 and w_2 be values of a_1 and a_2 respectively, then w_1 and w_2 are defined to be i-level QI-Compatible if the following two conditions are satisfied: (1) a_1 and a_2 are QI-Compatible with respect to S, and (2) S consists of all quality indicators present within i levels of the quality indicator tree of a_1 (thus of a_2).

By the same token, i-level QIV-Equal between w_1 and w_2, denoted by $w_1 =^i w_2$, can be defined.

If 'i' is the maximum level of depth in the quality indicator tree, then a_1 and a_2 are defined to be maximum-level QI-Compatible. Similarly, maximum-level QIV-Equal between w_1 and w_2, denoted by $w_1 =^m w_2$, can also be defined.

16

To exemplify the algebraic operations in the quality indicator algebra, we introduce two quality relations having the same quality scheme set as shown in Figure 9. They are referred to as Large_and_Medium (Tables 7, 7.1, 7.2 in Figure 13) and Small_and_Medium (Tables 8, 8.1, and 8.2 in Figure 14).

	<CN, nil¢>	<CEO, nil¢>	<EE, EE¢>
Table 7	<IBM, nil¢>	<J Akers, nil¢>	<6.08, id0101¢>
	<DEC, nil¢>	<K Olsen, nil¢>	<-0.32, id0102¢>
	<TI, nil¢>	<J Junkins, nil¢>	<2.51, id0103¢>

	<EE¢, nil¢>	<SRC1, SRC1¢>	<Reporting_date, nil¢>
Table 7.1	<id0101¢, nil¢>	<Nexis, id0201¢>	<10-07-92, nil¢>
	<id0102¢, nil¢>	<Nexis, id0202¢>	<10-07-92, nil¢>
	<id0103¢, nil¢>	<Lotus, id0203¢>	<10-07-92, nil¢>

	<SRC1¢, nil¢>	<SRC2, nil¢>	<Reporting_date, nil¢>
Table 7.2	<id0201¢, nil¢>	<Zacks, nil¢>	<1-07-92, nil¢>
	<id0202¢, nil¢>	<First Boston, nil¢>	<1-07-92, nil¢>
	<id0203¢, nil¢>	<First Boston, nil¢>	<1-07-92, nil¢>

Figure 13: The Quality Relation Large_and_Medium

	<CN, nil¢>	<CEO, nil¢>	<EE, EE¢>
Table 8	<Apple, nil¢>	<J Sculley, nil¢>	<5.69, id1101¢>
	<DEC, nil¢>	<K Olsen, nil¢>	<-0.32, id1102¢>
	<TI, nil¢>	<J Junkins, nil¢>	<2.51, id1103¢>

	<EE¢, nil>	<SRC1, SRC1¢>	<Reporting_date, nil¢>
Table 8.1	<id1101¢, nil¢>	<Lotus, id1201¢>	<10-07-92, nil¢>
	<id1102¢, nil¢>	<Nexis, id1202¢>	<10-07-92, nil¢>
	<id1103¢, nil¢>	<Lotus, id1203¢>	<10-07-92, nil¢>

	<SRC1¢, nil¢>	<SRC2, nil¢>	<Reporting_date, nil¢>
Table 8.2	<id1201¢, nil¢>	<Zacks, nil¢>	<1-07-92, nil¢>
	<id1202¢, nil¢>	<First Boston, nil¢>	<1-07-92, nil¢>
	<dd1203¢, nil¢>	<Zacks, nil¢>	<1-07-92, nil¢>

Figure 14: The Quality Relation Small_and_Medium

These two quality relations will be used to illustrate various operations of the quality indicator algebra. In order to illustrate the relationship between the quality indicator algebraic operations and the high-level user query, the SELECT, FROM, WHERE structure of SQL is extended with an extra clause "with QUALITY." This extra clause enables a user to specify the quality requirements regarding an attributes referred to in a query.

17

If the clause "with QUALITY" is absent in a user query, then it means that the user has no explicit constraints on the quality of data that is being retrieved. In that case quality indicator values would not be compared in the retrieval process, however, the quality indicator values associated with the applications data would be retrieved as well

In the extended SQL syntax, the dot notation is used to identify a quality indicator in the quality indicator tree. In Figure 9, for example, EE SRC1 SRC2 identifies SRC2 which is a quality indicator for SRC1, which in turn is a quality indicator to EE

The quality indicator algebra is presented in the following subsection

4 3 2. Quality Indicator Algebra

Following the relational algebra (Klug, 1982), we define the five orthogonal quality relational algebraic operations, namely selection, projection, union, difference, and Cartesian product

In the following operations, let QR and QS be two quality schemes and let qr and qs be two quality relations associated with QR and QS respectively. Let a and b be two attributes in both QR and QS. Let t_1 and t_2 be two quality tuples. Let S_a be a set of quality indicators specified by the user for the attribute a. (That is, S_a is constructed form the specifications given by the user in the "with QUALITY" clause.) Let the term $t_1 a = t_2 a$ denote that the values of the attribute a in the tuples t_1 and t_2 are identical. Let $t_1 a =^{S_a} t_2 a$ denote that the values of attribute a in the tuples t_1 and t_2 are QIV-equal with respect to S_a. Similarly, let $t_1 a =^1 t_2 a$ and $t_1 a =^m t_2 a$ denote 1-level QIV-equal and maximum-level QIV-equal respectively between the values of $t_1 a$ and $t_2 a$

4 3 2 1 Selection

Selection is a unary operation which selects only a horizontal subset of a quality relation (and its corresponding quality indicator relations) based on the conditions specified in the Selection operation. There are two types of conditions in the Selection operation: regular conditions for an application attribute and quality conditions for the quality indicator relations corresponding to the application attribute. The selection, $\sigma^q_C (qr)$, is defined as follows

$$\sigma^q_C (qr) = \{t \mid \forall t_1 \in qr, \ \forall a \in QR, ((t.a = t_1 a) \land (t a =^m t_1 a)) \land C(t_1)\}$$

where $C(t_1) = e_1 \Phi e_2 \Phi \quad \Phi e_n \Phi e_1^q \Phi e_2^q \Phi \quad \Phi e_p^q$, e_i is in one of the forms: $(t_1 a \ \theta \ \text{constant})$ or $(t_1 a \ \theta \ t_1 b)$, e_i^q is of the forms $(qi_k = \text{constant})$ or $(t_1 a =^{S_{a,b}} t_1 b)$ or $(t_1 a =^1 t_1 b)$ or $(t_1 a =^m t_1 b)$, $qi_k \in QI(a)$, $\Phi \in \{\land, \lor, \neg\}$, $\theta = \{\leq, \geq, \leq, \neq, <, >, =\}$, and $S_{a,b}$ is the set of quality indicators to be compared during the comparison of $t_1 a$ and $t_1 b$

18

<u>Example 1</u>: Get all Large_and_Medium companies whose earnings estimate is over 2 and is supplied by

Zacks Investment Research.

A corresponding extended SQL query is shown as follows:

SELECT	CN, CEO, EE
FROM	LARGE_AND_MEDIUM
WHERE	EE > 2
with **QUALITY**	EE.SRC1.SRC2='Zacks'

This SQL query can be accomplished through a Selection operation in the quality indicator

algebra. The result is shown below.

	<CN, nil¢>	<CEO, nil¢>	<EE, EE¢>
Table 9	<IBM, nil¢>	<J Akers, nil¢>	<6.08, id0101¢>

	<EE¢, nil¢>	<SRC1, SRC1¢>	<Reporting_date, nil¢>
Table 9.1	<id0101¢, nil¢>	<Nexis, id0201¢>	<10-07-92, nil¢>

	<SRC1¢, nil¢>	<SRC2, nil¢>	<Reporting_date, nil¢>
Table 9.2	<id0201¢, nil¢>	<Zacks, nil¢>	<1-07-92, nil¢>

Note that in the conventional relational model, only Table 9 would be produced as a result of

this SQL query. Whereas, in the quality indicator algebra, Tables 9.1, 9.2 are also produced. Table 9

shows that the earnings estimate for IBM is 6.08; and the quality indicator values in Tables 9.1 and 9.2

show that the data is retrieved from the Nexis database on October 7, 1992, which, in turn, is based on

data reported by Zacks Investment Research on January 7, 1992. An experienced user could infer from

these quality indicator values that the estimate is credible, given that Zacks is a reliable source of

earnings estimates.

4.3.2.2. Projection

Projection is a unary operation which selects a vertical subset of a quality relation based on the

set of attributes specified in the Projection operation. The result includes the projected quality relation

and the corresponding quality indicator relations that are associated with the set of attributes

specified in the Projection operation.

Let PJ be the attribute set specified, then the Projection, $\Pi^q_{PJ}(qr)$, is defined as follows:

$$\Pi^q_{PJ}(qr) = \{t \mid \forall\ t_1 \in qr,\ \forall a \in PJ,\ ((t.a = t_1.a) \wedge (t.a =^m t_1.a\ ))\}$$

<u>Example 2</u>: Get company names and earnings estimates of all Large_and_Medium companies

A corresponding SQL query is shown as follows:

19

SELECT   CN, EE
FROM LARGE_and MEDIUM

This SQL query can be accomplished through a Projection operation. The result is shown below.

<CN, nile>	<EE, EEc>
<IBM, nile>	<6.08, id0101c>
<DEC, nile>	<-0.32, id0102c>
<TI, nile>	<2.51, id0103c>

<EEc, nile>	<SRC1, SRC1c>	<Reporting_date, nile>
<id0101c, nile>	<Nexis, id0201c>	<10-07-92, nile>
<id0102c, nile>	<Nexis, id0202c>	<10-07-92, nile>
<id0103c, nile>	<Lotus, id0203c>	<10-07-92, nile>

<SRC1c, nile>	<SRC2, nile>	<Reporting_date, nile>
<id0201c, nile>	<Zacks, nile>	<1-07-92, nile>
<id0202c, nile>	<First Boston, nile>	<1-07-92, nile>
<id0203c, nile>	<First Boston, nile>	<1-07-92, nile>

4.3.2.3. Union

In Union, the two operand quality relations must be QI-Compatible. The result includes (1) tuples from both qr and qs after elimination of duplicates, and (2) the corresponding quality indicator relations that are associated with the resulting tuples.

$$qr \cup^q qs = qr \cup \{ t \mid \forall t_2 \in qs, \exists t_1 \in qr,$$
$$\forall a \in QR, ((t.a = t_2.a) \wedge (t.a =^m t_2.a) \wedge \neg ((t_1.a = t_2.a) \wedge (t_1.a =^{S_a} t_2.a)))\}$$

In the above expression, "$\neg (t_1.a = t_2.a \wedge t_1.a =^{S_a} t_2.a)$" is meant to eliminate duplicates. Tuples t_1 and t_2 are considered duplicates provided that (1) there is a match between their corresponding attribute values (i.e., $t_1.a = t_2.a$) and (2) these values are QIV-equal with respect to the set of quality indicators (S_a) specified by the user (i.e., $t_1.a =^{S_a} t_2.a$).

Example 3-1: Get company names, CEO names, and earnings estimates of all Large_and_Medium and Small_and_Medium companies.

A corresponding extended SQL query is shown as follows:

```
SELECT        LM.CN, LM.CEO, LM.EE
FROM          LARGE_and_MEDIUM  LM
UNION
SELECT        SM.CN, SM.CEO, SM.EE
FROM          SMALL_and_MEDIUM  SM
with QUALITY  (LM.EE.SRC1.SRC2= SM.EE.SRC1.SRC2)
```

This SQL query can be accomplished through a Union operation. The result is shown below.

<CN, nil¢>	<CEO, nil¢>	<EE, EE¢>
<IBM, nil¢>	<J Akers, nil¢>	<6.08, id0101¢>
<DEC, nil¢>	<K Olsen, nil¢>	<-0.32, id0102¢>
<TI, nil¢>	<J Junkins, nil¢>	<2.51, id0103¢>
<Apple, nil¢>	<J Sculley, nil¢>	<5.69, id1101¢>
<TI, nil¢>	<J Junkins, nil¢>	<2.51, id1103¢>

<EE¢, nil¢>	<SRC1, SRC1¢>	<Reporting_date, nil¢>
<id0101¢, nil¢>	<Nexis, id0201¢>	<10-07-92, nil¢>
<id0102¢, nil¢>	<Nexis, id0202¢>	<10-07-92, nil¢>
<id0103¢, nil¢>	<Lotus, id0203¢>	<10-07-92, nil¢>
<id1101¢, nil¢>	<Lotus, id1201¢>	<10-07-92, nil¢>
<id1103¢, nil¢>	<Lotus, id1203¢>	<10-07-92, nil¢>

<SRC1¢, nil¢>	<SRC2, nil¢>	<Reporting_date, nil¢>
<id0201¢, nil¢>	<Zacks, nil¢>	<1-07-92, nil¢>
<id0202¢, nil¢>	<First Boston, nil¢>	<1-07-92, nil¢>
<id0203¢, nil¢>	<First Boston, nil¢>	<1-07-92, nil¢>
<id1201¢, nil¢>	<Zacks, nil¢>	<1-07-92, nil¢>
<id1203¢, nil¢>	<Zacks, nil¢>	<1-07-92, nil¢>

Note that there are two tuples corresponding to the company TI in the result because their quality indicator values are different with respect to SRC2.

Example 3-2: If the quality requirement were (LM.EE.SRC1= SM.EE.SRC1) then these two tuples would be considered duplicates and only one tuple for TI is retained in the result. The result of this query is shown below:

<CN, nil¢>	<CEO, nil¢>	<EE, EE¢>
<IBM, nil¢>	<J Akers, nil¢>	<6.08, id0101¢>
<DEC, nil¢>	<K Olsen, nil¢>	<-0.32, id0102¢>
<TI, nil¢>	<J Junkins, nil¢>	<2.51, id0103¢>
<Apple, nil¢>	<J Sculley, nil¢>	<5.69, id1101¢>

<EE¢, nil¢>	<SRC1, SRC1¢>	<Reporting_date, nil¢>
<id0101¢, nil¢>	<Nexis, id0201¢>	<10-07-92, nil¢>
<id0102¢, nil¢>	<Nexis, id0202¢>	<10-07-92, nil¢>
<id0103¢, nil¢>	<Lotus, id0203¢>	<10-07-92, nil¢>
<id1101¢, nil¢>	<Lotus, id1201¢>	<10-07-92, nil¢>

<SRC1¢, nil¢>	<SRC2, nil¢>	<Reporting_date, nil¢>
<id0201¢, nil¢>	<Zacks, nil¢>	<1-07-92, nil¢>
<id0202¢, nil¢>	<First Boston, nil¢>	<1-07-92, nil¢>
<id0203¢, nil¢>	<First Boston, nil¢>	<1-07-92, nil¢>
<id1201¢, nil¢>	<Zacks, nil¢>	<1-07-92, nil¢>

Note also that unlike the relational union, the quality union operation is not commutative. This is illustrated in Example 3-3 below.

Example 3-3: Consider the following extended SQL query which switches the order of the union operation in Example 3-b:

```
SELECT        SM.CN, SM.CEO, SM.EE
FROM          SMALL_and_MEDIUM  SM
UNION
SELECT        LM.CN, LM.CEO, LM.EE
FROM          LARGE_and_MEDIUM  LM
with QUALITY  (LM.EE.SRC1= SM.EE.SRC1)
```

The result is shown below.

<CN, nil$e$>	<CEO, nil$e$>	<EE, EEe>
<IBM, nil$e$>	<J Akers, nil$e$>	<6.08, id0101e>
<DEC, nil$e$>	<K Olsen, nil$e$>	<-0.32, id0102e>
<Apple, nil$e$>	<J Sculley, nil$e$>	<5.69, id1101e>
<TI, nil$e$>	<J Junkins, nil$e$>	<2.51, id1103e>

<EEe, nil$e$>	<SRC1, SRC1e>	<Reporting_date, nil$e$>
<id0101e, nil$e$>	<Nexis, id0201e>	<10-07-92, nil$e$>
<id0102e, nil$e$>	<Nexis, id0202e>	<10-07-92, nil$e$>
<id1101e, nil$e$>	<Lotus, id1201e>	<10-07-92, nil$e$>
<id1103e, nil$e$>	<Lotus, id1203e>	<10-07-92, nil$e$>

<SRC1e, nil$e$>	<SRC2, nil$e$>	<Reporting_date, nil$e$>
<id0201e, nil$e$>	<Zacks, nil$e$>	<1-07-92, nil$e$>
<id0202e, nil$e$>	<First Boston, nil$e$>	<1-07-92, nil$e$>
<id1201e, nil$e$>	<Zacks, nil$e$>	<1-07-92, nil$e$>
<id1202e, nil$e$>	<Zacks, nil$e$>	<1-07-92, nil$e$>

In the above result the tuple corresponding to TI is taken from SMALL_and_MEDIUM companies. On the other hand, in Example 3-2 it is taken from the LARGE_and_MEDIUM companies.

4.3.2.4. Difference

In Difference, the two operand quality relations must be QI-Compatible. The result of this operation consists of all tuples from qr which are not equal to tuples in qs. During this equality test the quality of attributes specified by the user for each attribute value in the tuples t_1 and t_2 will also be taken into consideration.

$$qr -^q qs = \{ t \mid \forall t_1 \in qr, \exists t_2 \in qs,$$

$$\forall a \in QR, ((t.a = t_1.a) \wedge (t.a =^m t_1.a) \wedge \neg ((t_1.a = t_2.a) \wedge (t_1.a =^{Sa} t_2.a)))\}$$

22

Example 4: Get all the companies which are classified as only Large_and_Medium companies but not as Small_and_Medium companies.

A corresponding SQL query is shown as follows:

```
SELECT       LM.CN, LM.CEO, LM.EE
FROM         LARGE_and_MEDIUM LM
DIFFERENCE
SELECT       SM.CN, SM.CEO, SM.EE
FROM         SMALL_and_MEDIUM SM
with QUALITY (LM.EE.SRC1.SRC2 = SM.EE.SRC1.SRC2)
```

This SQL query can be accomplished through a Difference operation. The result is shown below.

<CN, nil>	<CEO, nil¢>	<EE, EE>
<IBM, nil¢>	<J Akers, nil¢>	<6.08, id0101¢>
<TI, nil¢>	<J Junkins, nil¢>	<2.51, id0103¢>

<EE¢, nil>	<SRC1, SRC1¢>	<Reporting_date, nil¢>
<id0101¢, nil¢>	<Nexis, id0201¢>	<10-07-92, nil¢>
<id0103¢, nil¢>	<Lotus, id0203¢>	<10-07-92, nil¢>

<SRC1¢, nil>	<SRC2, nil¢>	<Reporting_date, nil¢>
<id0201¢, nil¢>	<Zacks, nil¢>	<1-07-92, nil¢>
<id0203¢, nil¢>	<Zacks, nil¢>	<1-07-92, nil¢>

Note here that according to the conventional relational algebra, the tuple corresponding to the company TI must not be included in the result. But in quality indicator algebra the tuple corresponding to the company TI from the relation Large_and_Medium is included in the result because the corresponding tuple in the relation Small_and_Medium has different quality indicators than those of the relation Large_and_Medium. In the following paragraph, an example is provided to demonstrate the change in the contents of results when quality requirements changes.

If the constraint in the QUALITY part of the query were (LM.EE.SRC1 = SM.EE.SRC1) then the result is as follows:

<CN, nil¢>	<CEO, nil¢>	<EE, EE¢>
<IBM, nil¢>	<J Akers, nil¢>	<6.08, id0101¢>

<EE¢, nil¢>	<SRC1, SRC1¢>	<Reporting_date, nil¢>
<id0101¢, nil¢>	<Nexis, id0201¢>	<10-07-92, nil¢>

<SRC1¢, nil¢>	<SRC2, nil¢>	<Reporting_date, nil¢>
<id0201¢, nil¢>	<Zacks, nil¢>	<1-07-92, nil¢>

23

4.3.2.5. Cartesian Product

The Cartesian product is also a binary operation. Let QR be of degree r and QS be of degree s. Let $t_1 \in qr$ $t_2 \in qs$. Let $t_1(i)$ denote the ith attribute of the tuple t_1 and $t_2(i)$ denote the ith attribute of the tuple t_2. The tuple t in the quality relation resulting from the Cartesian product of qr and qs will be of degree r+s. The Cartesian product of qr and qs, denoted as qr X^q qs, is defined as follows:

$$qr \ X^q \ qs = \{ t \mid \forall t_1 \in qr, \forall t_2 \in qs,$$

$$t(1) = t_1(1) \wedge t(1) =^m t_1(1) \wedge \ t(2) = t_1(2) \wedge t(2) =^m t_1(2) \wedge \ ... \ t(r) = t_1(r) \wedge t(r) =^m t_1(r) \wedge$$

$$t(r+1) = t_2(1) \wedge t(r+1) =^m t_2(1) \wedge \ t(r+2) = t_2(2) \wedge t(r+2) =^m t_2(2) \wedge \ ... \ t(r+s) = t_2(s) \wedge t(r+s) =^m t_2(s) \}$$

The result of the Cartesian product between Large_and_Medium and Small_and_Medium is shown below.

\<LM.CN, nile\>	\<LM.CEO, nile\>	\<LM.EE, EEe\>	\<SM.CN, nile\>	\<SM.CEO, nile\>	\<SM.EE, EEe\>
\<IBM, nile\>	\<J Akers, nile\>	\<6.08,id0101e\>	\<Apple,nile\>	\<J Sculley, nile\>	\<5.69, id1101e\>
\<IBM, nile\>	\<J Akers, nile\>	\<6.08,id0101e\>	\<DEC, nile\>	\<K Olsen, nile\>	\<-0.32, id1102e\>
\<IBM, nile\>	\<J Akers, nile\>	\<6.08,id0101e\>	\<TI, nile\>	\<J Junkins, nile\>	\<2.51, id1103e\>
\<DEC, nile\>	\<K Olsen, nile\>	\<-0.32,id0102e\>	\<Apple, nile\>	\<J Sculley, nile\>	\<5.69, id1101e\>
\<DEC, nile\>	\<K Olsen, nile\>	\<-0.32,id0102e\>	\<DEC, nile\>	\<K Olsen, nile\>	\<-0.32, id1102e\>
\<DEC, nile\>	\<K Olsen, nile\>	\<-0.32,id0102e\>	\<TI, nile\>	\<J Junkins, nile\>	\<2.51, id1103e\>
\<TI, nile\>	\<J Junkins, nile\>	\<2.51,id0103e\>	\<Apple, nile\>	\<J Sculley, nile\>	\<5.69, id1101e\>
\<TI, nile\>	\<J Junkins, nile\>	\<2.51,id0103e\>	\<DEC, nile\>	\<K Olsen, nile\>	\<-0.32, id1102e\>
\<TI, nile\>	\<J Junkins, nile\>	\<2.51,id0103e\>	\<TI, nile\>	\<J Junkins, nile\>	\<2.51, id1103e\>

\<LM.EEe, nile\>	\<LM.SRC1, SRC1e\>	\<LM.Reporting_date,nile\>
\<id0101e, nile\>	\<Nexis, d0201e\>	\<10-07-92,nile\>
\<id0102e, nile\>	\<Lotus, id0202e\>	\<10-07-92,nile\>
\<id0103e, nile\>	\<Nexis, id0203e\>	\<10-07-92,nile\>

\<LM.SRC1e, nile\>	\<LM.SRC2, nile\>	\<LM.Reporting_date,nile\>
\<id0201e, nile\>	\<Zacks,nile\>	\<1-07-92,nile\>
\<id0202e, nile\>	\<First Boston,nile\>	\<1-07-92,nile\>
\<id0203e, nile\>	\<First Boston,nile\>	\<1-07-92,nile\>

\<SM.EEe, nil\>	\<SM.SRC1, SRC1e\>	\<SM.Reporting_date, nile\>
\<id1101e, nile\>	\<Lotus, id1201e\>	\<10-07-92, nile\>
\<id1102e, nile\>	\<Nexis, id1202e\>	\<10-07-92, nile\>
\<id1103e, nile\>	\<Lotus, id1203e\>	\<10-07-92, nile\>

\<SM.SRC1e, nile\>	\<SM.SRC2, nile\>	\<SM.Reporting_date, nile\>
\<id1201e, nile\>	\<Zacks, nile\>	\<1-07-92, nile\>
\<id1202e, nile\>	\<First Boston, nile\>	\<1-07-92, nile\>
\<id1203e, nile\>	\<Zacks, nile\>	\<1-07-92, nile\>

The set of quality indicator tables associated with each attribute in the table resulting from the Cartesian product are retrieved as part of the result.

Other algebraic operators such as Intersection and Join can be derived from these five orthogonal operators, as does in the relational algebra.

24

We have presented the attribute-based model including a description of the model structure, a set of integrity constraints for the model, and a quality indicator algebra   In addition, each of the algebraic operations are exemplified in the context of the SQL query   The next section discusses some of the capabilities of this model and future research directions

5.   Discussion and future directions

The attribute-based model can be applied in many different ways and some of them are listed below

- The ability of the model to support quality indicators at multiple levels makes it possible to retain the origin and intermediate data sources   The example in Figure 9 illustrates this

- A user can filter the data retrieved from a database   according to quality requirements   In Example 1, for instance, only the data furnished by Zacks Investment Research is retrieved as specified in the clause "with QUALITY   EE SRC1 SRC2='Zacks' "

- Data authenticity and believability can be improved by data inspection and certification   A quality indicator value could indicate who inspected or certified the data and when it was inspected   The reputation of the inspector will enhance the believability of the data

- The quality indicators associated with data can help clarify data semantics, which can be used to resolve semantic incompatibility among data items received from different sources   This capability is very useful in an interoperable environment where data in different databases have different semantics

- Quality indicators associated with an attribute may facilitate a better interpretation of null values   For example, if the value retrieved for the spouse field is empty in an employee record, it can be interpreted (i e , tagged) in several ways, such as (1) the employee is unmarried, (2) the spouse name is unknown, or (3) this tuple is inserted into the employee table from the materialization of a view over a table which does not have spouse field

- In a data quality control process, when errors are detected, the data administrator can identify the source of error by examining quality indicators such as data source or collection method

In this paper, we have investigated how quality indicators may be specified, stored, retrieved, and processed   Specifically, we have (1) established a step-by-step procedure for data quality requirements analysis and specification, (2) presented a model for the structure, storage, and processing

25

of quality relations and quality indicator relations (through the algebra), and (3) touched upon functionalities related to data quality administration and control

We are actively pursuing research in the following areas (1) In order to determine the quality of derived data (e g , combining accurate monthly data with less accurate weekly data), we are investigating mechanisms to determine the quality of derived data based on the quality indicator values of its components (2) In order to use this model for existing databases, which do not have tagging capability, they must be extended with quality schemas instantiated with appropriate quality indicator values We are exploring the possibility of making such a transformation cost-effective (3) Though we have chosen the relational model to represent the quality schema, an object-oriented approach appears natural to model data and its quality indicators Because many of the quality control mechanisms are procedure oriented and o-o models can handle procedures (i e , methods), we are investigating the pros and cons of the object-oriented approach

6. References

[1] Ballou, D P & Pazer, H L (1985) Modeling Data and Process Quality in Multi-input, Multi-output Information Systems *Management Science, 31*(2), pp 150-162

[2] Ballou, D P & Pazer, H L (1987). Cost/Quality Tradeoffs for Control Procedures in Information Systems *International Journal of Management Science, 15*(6), pp 509-521

[3] Batini, C, Lenzirini, M, & Navathe, S (1986) A comparative analysis of methodologies for database schema integration *ACM Computing Survey, 18*(4), pp 323 - 364

[4] Codd, E F (1970) A relational model of data for large shared data banks *Communications of the ACM, 13*(6), pp 377-387

[5] Codd, E F. (1979) Extending the relational database model to capture more meaning *ACM Transactions on Database Systems, 4*(4), pp 397-434

[6] Codd, E F (1982) Relational database. A practical foundation for productivity, the 1981 ACM Turing Award Lecture *Communications of the ACM, 25*(2), pp 109-117

[7] Date, C J (1990) *An Introduction to Database Systems* (5th ed) Reading, MA Addison-Wesley

[8] Garvin, D A (1983) Quality on the line *Harvard Business Review*, (September- October), pp 65-75

[9] Garvin, D A (1987) Competing on the eight dimensions of quality *Harvard Business Review*, (November-December), pp 101-109

[10] Garvin, D A (1988) *Managing Quality-The Strategic and Competitive Edge* (1 ed) New York The Free Press

[11] Huh, Y U , et al (1990) Data Quality *Information and Software Technology, 32*(8), pp 559-565

[12] Johnson, J R, Leitch, R A, & Neter, J (1981) Characteristics of Errors in Accounts Receivable and Inventory Audits *Accounting Review, 56*(April), pp 270-293

[13] Juran, J M (1979) *Quality Control Handbook* (3rd ed) New York McGraw-Hill Book Co

[14] Juran, J M & Gryna, F M (1980) *Quality Planning and Analysis* (2nd ed) New York McGraw Hill

[15] Khoshafian, S N & Copeland, G P (1990) Object Identity In S B Zdonik& D Maier (Ed), (pp 37-46) San Mateo, CA Morgan Kaufmann

[16] Klug, A (1982) Equivalence of relational algebra and relational calculus query languages having aggregate functions *The Journal of ACM, 29*, pp 699-717

[17] Laudon, K C (1986) Data Quality and Due Process in Large Interorganizational Record Systems *Communications of the ACM, 29*(1), pp 4-11.

[18] Liepins, G E. & Uppulun, V R R. (1990) *Data Quality Control Theory and Pragmatics* (pp 360) New York Marcel Dekker, Inc

[19] Liepins, O E (1989). Sound Data Are a Sound Investment *Quality Programs*, (September), pp 61-63

[20] Maier, D (1983) *The Theory of Relational Databases* (1st ed) Rockville, MD. Computer Science Press

[21] McCarthy, J L (1982) *Metadata Management for Large Statistical Databases* Mexico City, Mexico 1982 pp 234-243

[22] McCarthy, J L (1984) *Scientific Information = Data + Meta-data* U S Naval Postgraduate School, Monterey, CA 1984 pp

[23] McCarthy, J L (1988) *The Automated Data Thesaurus A New Tool for Scientific Information* Proceedings of the 11th International Codata Conference, Karlsruhe, Germany 1988 pp

[24] Morey, R C (1982) Estimating and Improving the Quality of Information in the MIS *Communications of the ACM*, 25(May), pp 337-342

[25] Navathe, S, Batini, C, & Ceri, S (1992) *The Entity Relationship Approach* New york Wiley and Sons

[26] Rockart, J F & Short, J E (1989) IT in the 1990s Managing Organizational Interdependence *Sloan Management Review, Sloan School of Management, MIT*, 30(2), pp 7-17

[27] Sciore, E (1991) Using Annotations to Support Multiple Kinds of Versioning in an Object-Oriented Database System. *ACM Transactions on Database Systems*, 16(No 3, September 1991), pp 417-438

[28] Siegel, M & Madnick, S E (1991) *A metadata approach to resolving semantic conflicts* Barcelona, Spain 1991 pp

[29] Teorey, T J. (1990) *Database Modeling and Design The Entity-Relationship Approach* San Mateo, CA Morgan Kaufman Publisher

[30] Wang, R Y & Kon, H B (1992) Towards Total Data Quality Management (TDQM) In R Y Wang (Ed), *Information Technology in Action Trends and Perspectives* Englewood Cliffs, NJ Prentice Hall

[31] Wang, Y R & Guarrascio, L M (1991) *Dimensions of Data Quality Beyond Accuracy* (CISL-91-06) Composite Information Systems Laboratory, Sloan School of Management, Massachusetts Institute of Technology, Cambridge, MA, 02139 June 1991

[32] Wang, Y. R & Madnick, S E (1990) *A Polygen Model for Heterogeneous Database Systems The Source Tagging Perspective* Brisbane, Australia 1990 pp 519-538

[33] Zarkovich (1966) *Quality of Statistical Data* Rome Food and Agriculture Organization of the United Nations

7. Appendix A: Premises about data quality requirements analysis

Below we present premises related to data quality modeling and data quality requirements analysis. To facilitate further discussion, we define a _data quality attribute_ as a collective term that refers to both quality parameters and quality indicators as shown in Figure A.1. (This term is referred to as a _quality attribute_ hereafter.)

Figure A.1: Relationship among quality attributes, quality parameters, and quality indicators.

7.1. Premises related to data quality modeling

Data quality modeling is an extension of traditional data modeling methodologies. As data modeling captures many of the structural and semantic issues underlying data, data quality modeling captures many of the structural and semantic issues underlying data quality. The following four premises relate to these data quality modeling issues.

(Premise 1.1) (Relatedness between entity and quality attributes): In some cases a quality attribute can be considered either as an entity attribute (i.e., an application entity's attribute) or as a quality attribute. For example, the name of a teller who performs a transaction in a banking application may be an entity attribute if initial application requirements state that the teller's name be included; alternatively, it may be modeled as a quality attribute.

From a modeling perspective, whether an attribute should be modeled as an entity attribute or a quality attribute is a judgment call on the part of the design team, and may depend on the initial application requirements as well as eventual uses of the data, such as the inspection of the data for distribution to external users, or for integration with other data of different quality. The relevance of distribution and integration of the information is that often the users of a given system "know" the quality of the data they use. When the data is exported to their users, however, or combined with information of different quality, that quality may become unknown.

A guideline to this judgment is to ask what information the attribute provides. If the attribute provides application information such as a customer name and address, it may be considered an entity attribute. If, on the other hand, the information relates more to aspects of the data manufacturing process, such as when, where, and by whom the data was manufactured, then this may be a quality attribute.

In short, the objective of the data quality requirement analysis is not strictly to develop quality attributes, but also to ensure that important dimensions of data quality are not overlooked entirely in requirement analysis.

(Premise 1 2) (Quality attribute non-orthogonality) Different quality attributes need not be orthogonal to one another For example, the two quality parameters *credibility* and *timeliness* are related (i e , not orthogonal), such as for real time data

(Premise 1 3) (Heterogeneity and hierarchy in the quality of supplied data) Quality of data may differ across databases, entities, attributes, and instances Database example information in a university database may be of higher quality than data in John Doe's personal database Entity example data about alumni (an entity) may be less reliable than data about students (an entity) Attribute example in the student entity, grades may be more accurate than are addresses Instance example data about an international student may be less interpretable than that of a domestic student

7.2. Premises related to data quality definitions and standards across users

Because human insight is needed for data quality modeling and different people may have different opinions regarding data quality, different quality definitions and standards may result We call this phenomenon "data quality is in the eye of the beholder " The following two premises entail this phenomenon

(Premise 2 1) (Users define different quality attributes) Quality parameters and quality indicators may vary from one user to another Quality parameter example for a manager the quality parameter for a research report may be inexpensive, whereas for a financial trader, the research report may need to be credible and timely Quality indicator example. the manager may measure inexpensiveness in terms of the quality indicator (monetary) cost, whereas the trader may measure inexpensiveness in terms of opportunity cost of her own time and thus the quality indicator may be retrieval time

(Premise 2 2) (Users have different quality standards) Acceptable levels of data quality may differ from one user to another. For example, an investor following the movement of a stock may consider a fifteen minute delay for share price to be sufficiently timely, whereas a trader who needs price quotes in real time may not consider fifteen minutes to be timely enough

7.3. Premises related to a single user

A single user may have different quality attributes and quality standards for the different data used This phenomenon is summarized in Premise 3 below

(Premise 3) (For a single user, non-uniform data quality attributes and standards). A user may have different quality attributes and quality standards across databases, entities, attributes, or instances Across attributes example A user may need higher quality information for the phone number than for the number of employees Across instances example A user may need high quality information for certain companies, but not for others due to the fact that some companies are of particular interest

www.ingramcontent.com/pod-product-compliance
Lightning Source LLC
LaVergne TN
LVHW012201040326
832903LV00003B/45